COPYCAT RECIPES:
FAST FOOD COOKBOOK

30+ FAST FOOD CLONE RECIPES OF
THE MOST POPULAR BRAND.

DISCOVER COPYCAT FAST FOOD RECIPES
AND FEEL LIKE YOU ARE EATING OUT IN
YOUR OWN KITCHEN.

DEDICATION

This book is dedicated to Almighty God who has been the pillar of my life; my helper, sufficiency and source of strength.

I would also like to dedicate this book to my wonderful mother for her understanding and support for standing by me through the years.

CONTENT

INTRODUCTION

It has been discovered that a vast amount of we people delight in eating most meals at our favorite restaurant; However, survey shows that the expense of getting this sumptuous dishes now are way higher than they were before, due to some limitations labelled on us and economic constraints. If you happen to be one of those people who fall under this category; then why not treat your loved ones with the favorite dishes you so much enjoy and pay a great sum for, just exactly the same way its been prepared and served at your favorite restaurants, by making it at home, in your own kitchen. Sounds AWESOME, right?

This book pays off immediately you start putting it to use, because you get to cook your favourite special delicacies at home, at a much lower and minimal food costs. In this well organised book, you will find instructions for each of the fantastic dishes people buy at various restaurant, and be rest assured, feeling more secured than ever that the food is been cooked in the healthiest way possible and clean conditions. The only differences is you will be the one doing the cooking this time around.

The great thing about the Copycat Recipe cook book is you dont have to be an expert with some years of cooking experience to prepare this dishes. All the recipes provided in this book is prepared by the use of the basic ingredients available in any supermarket. There is no compelling reason to buy luxurious cooking device because the cooking procedures are very SIMPLE.

Also in this book, you will find tips on the best ways on how to make several unique restaurant special dishes simultaneously at the expense of your kitchen. You will also get a brief list of the basic cooking utensils that you will need in your kitchen. You will learn how to store ingredients for availability when preparing some amazing dishes and will be provided with a presentation of the most experienced methods in choosing the best and freshest ingredients. In the same way, you get the basic cooking conditions used in this book.

Copycat recipes can be a fun activity for the whole family. Your dining table will be filled with varieties of amazing dishes prepared at a much lower cost. You can now have your friends or families come over, or throw that little party knowing you have your cooking covered to delight your guests. There is no doubt you will be pleased with your meals because this book integrates various restaurant recipes into your food collection. You get to become a cook genius yourself.

CHAPTER 1:

THE COPYCAT COOKING WORLD

Anywhere your preferences are at this point in time, it would not be hard to find ingredients of most restaurant recipes. With a little work and a visit to the nearest market, you can serve dishes that no one can handle. You will be surprised at the investment you make when you use a restaurant recipes instead of eating at the same restaurant.

If you tend to host a party or a gathering, you can cook up recipes from restaurant that will make your guest believe that you bought it at a restaurant in which the dishes are popularly known for. This will make you appreciate the attention your kitchen will attract if you choose to make copies of restaurant recipes for your next gathering or party.

Just because you cook yourself doesn't mean it isn't as fun as a five-star restaurant. All you need is a few simple procedures. You don't have to be a master chef or a cooking expert. The equipment used to make recipes in this book is divided into cookware, cooking utensils, cooking devices and bakeware. In the same way, you will be familiarized with the conditions and procedures that are expected to produce exceptional food for restaurant quality.

COOKING DEVICES

These facilities offers the best comfort and adaptability in your kitchen:

Blender - This kitchen device cuts time in a fraction of a second by mixing, cutting and combining food ingredients.

Deep Fryer - This is best used to control the temperature of oil when frying foods such as meat and fishes

Electric mixer - A compact handheld device that can process ingredients in the kitchen with ease.

Indoor grill - This is of great help in the kitchen when roasting or grilling food in any form because both sides are cooked twice.

Microwave - As always, you can count on it to quickly warm and heat food in the kitchen.

COOKING UTENSILS

A good cook realizes that a proper knife arrangement in the kitchen can do more than any electronic device. These are the set of knives you need in the kitchen:

Chef knives

With wide and narrow shapes that no doubt can be cut through all ingredients.

Bread knives

Ideal for cutting food crusts.

Paring knives

It has short cutting edges that are used for peeling, cutting, and removing seeds from vegetables

Other utensils needed to prepare food include:
- Chopping board
- Colander
- Fork and spoon
- Grater
- Shaper (for pizza)
- Mallet (for meat)
- Openers for cans and tins
- Measuring spoons (tablespoons, tbsps. and teaspoons, tsps.)
- Measuring cup
- Knives
- Spatula
- Mixing bowls

Cooking in the kitchen can be fun, but it's still a place for possible accidents. There are some basic safety rules that you need to follow to make your cooking experience more enjoyable: It is important to understand your equipment and handle it properly. Always make sure to read the instructions on the most experienced ways to use your device.

COOKWARES
You also need several sets of cookware and they are:
- Saucepan with lid (small, medium, and large)
- Pots of various sizes
- Stockpot (big enough to make soup)
- Cast iron pan (used in the oven)
- Frying pan

BAKEWARES

These are some important baking devices used in the kitchen:

- Aluminum foil for baking.
- Casserole dishes (small, medium and large)
- Pans (rectangular) for baking cakes
- Pizza dishes
- Baking pan rack
- Muffin pan

INGREDIENTS STORAGE

Cooking is much easier if you have a view of the ingredients available, so you don't have to rush to the market every time you want to cook. Storage availability is an advantage for the cook. Here are some of the main ingredients that must be in the cupboard. Of course, you can adjust the product at the end to your preferences.

Herbs and Spices

If you have been to the spice market, you can see how expensive various spices are. A small bottle of spice costs two or three dollars. Therefore, it is recommended to buy a spice mix. The spices and seasonings that are known and widespread are:

- *Barbeque and grill spices*

They contain different flavors that can be sprinkled on the meat before roasting or grilling.

- *Cajun spice*

It is a mixture of paprika, garlic, onions, salt and pepper, which gives each dish a spicy taste.

- *Italian spices*

It is the most popular blend of basil and oregano, which is very essential in most pasta dishes.

- *Lemon pepper spice*

It gives a delicious taste to diaries and vegetables.

- *Mexican spices*

It contains a mixture of paprika, garlic, salt, and cumin, which are suitable for tacos, fajitas, and enchiladas.

The best way to fill your cabinet with spices is to buy a few new ones every time you go to town and buy new spices when needed.

SAUCES

Sauce is a great way to add flavor to your dish. Here are some sauces that you must have in the kitchen:

- Barbecue and grill sauce
- Bean stew sauce
- Chilli and hot pepper sauce
- Dried onion mixes
- Salad dressing mixes

- Soy sauce
- Canned soup (mushroom, chicken and celery soup)
- Steak sauce
- Sour and sweet sauce
- Teriyaki sauce
- Vinegar (red, rice and balsamic)
- Wine (red and white)

GROCERIES

You will also need some groceries that you will use repeatedly in different recipes. The basic elements for this kitchen include:

- Beans (various types of cans and dried)
- Oil (olive or veggie oil)
- Meat (beef, chicken, mutton and pork)
- Fishes and seafood
- Olives (dark and green)
- Pasta (mixed varieties)
- Rice (white, brown, long and wild)
- salsa
- Tomatoes (canned, tomato paste, ketchup and sauce)

BAKING PRODUCTS

To bake like the best restaurants do, you need to store a few basic ingredients in your cabinet, including:

- Baking mixes

- Baking powder
- Baking soda
- Beans (various types)
- Brown sugar
- Cornstarch
- Cocoa powder
- Flour
- Honey
- Pancakes mixes
- Seasoning chips (chocolate, peanut seals, caramel)
- Sugar
- Whole milk
- Yeast

DESSERT INGREDIENTS

To make many exotic restaurant desserts you need the following:

- Fruit slices
- Mixes for cakes, brownies and icing
- Ice cream mixes
- Pudding

PRODUCT TO BE REFRIGERATED

Store some useful products in the fridge so you can prepare your favorite copycat recipe without always having to go the store. Make a point of having:

- Mayonnaise
- Margarine or butter
- Tomato sauce
- Milk
- Cream
- Cheese (various types)
- Egg
- Mustard
- Salad cream
- Salad ingredients (various types of new vegetables)

PRODUCT TO BE FROZEN

There are some products, even if you don't use them all the time, you have to freeze them. They include:
- Chicken breast (skinless and boneless)
- Bread and pizza dough mixes
- Steak
- Baguettes
- Minced beef
- Vegetables (broccoli, spinach, pepper)

With these products, you can prepare beautiful and extraordinary food with a copy of the restaurant in a few moments. The thought that comes to your mind is which recipe should you try immediately.

CHOICE OF INGREDIENTS

Restaurant experts look for fresh ingredients that they can find so should you. Prepackages products should be studied whenever you can. Non-exclusive brands may offer lower prices but pay attention to quality and taste - you might not be satisfied with the final taste of the dish. By redesigning your methods, you can turn a standard diet into something extraordinary. For example, instead of using a certain mix and not just approving a type of cheese. Discover and experience new flavors.

MEATS

Red meat must have an attractive color and chicken must look full. Meat packaging must be in good shape without spills or excessive moisture. Check the expiration date and the instructions on the package to make sure the meat is new and has been processed properly. Freeze meat immediately after buying. Price is usually not an impression of value; Don't assume that the most expensive meat are the best, sort out quality.

Chicken

You can buy whole chickens or any package part such as wings, drumsticks and breast. When preparing chicken, care must be taken to maintain a strategic distance from cross contamination and salmonella. Wash hands and chicken before cooking. Remove the raw chicken from the others on the kitchen table in case of contamination. Use a different cutting board and knife only for raw chicken and do not use the same equipment for other purposes. If you follow these precautions, cooking with chicken is really great.

Beef

Beef contains no more than 30% fat, so the total amount of packaging expresses its fat content. Meet your butcher and specify the form you want it. Some cook or others roast beef for sale, let them grind the meat to get premium beef at a lower cost.

How do you identify the best type of beef from an ordinary beef? The products that you should look for when buying a beef are the slices and the quality. The quality evaluates animal age and meat size. The USDA considers the best beef a priority, followed by a decision and selection. When choosing beef, check the texture and the amount of fat flowing through the meat regularly. You need less fatty beef that produce the best taste. Beef slices are taken from various animal areas: the ribs; the legs and the abdominal regions

Always freeze your beef in the freezer for maximum preservation. Pay attention to safe handling on raw meat packaging labels. This will show you how to store, handle and cook meat safely.

Pork

When buying pork, look for slices with a limited amount of fat on the outside and meat with good colors and such as light-pink. For the best taste, pork must have a great shape. There are four main part in which pork slices are gotten are: legs, flank, shoulders and sides. From these slice you will get bacon, sausages, ribs, and ham.

FISH

Understanding how to choose fish is an experience that all chefs must have. Fresh fishes must have a smell like the type of water they came from. The eyes of the fish must be bright and clear, and the gills must be dark red. Don't buy it if it smells bad or looks spoilt.

FRUIT

When picking your fruits, pay attention to the softness, fullness and their colors. The fruit must be large and free of bites, slices, or other defects.

- Bananas are sold ripe and must be stored at the appropriate temperature.
- Fruits must be effectively isolated from the stems. Store them in the fridge at all costs.

- Melon with sweet scents must be chosen. A strong scents indicates that they are too ripe.
- Oranges, grapefruit, and lemons are sold when they are ripe. You can keep it in the refrigerator for 2-3 weeks.

VEGETABLES

Try to look at each vegetable carefully before you buy it. Make sure it looks fresh, soft, and colorful vegetables. Stay away from those who are wilted, dry, rotten, or damaged.

- Asparagus must have a conservative straight stem with a short tip.
- Brightly colored and fresh beans are your best choice.
- The light green and yellow head of broccoli should be avoided.
- Cabbage must have beautiful leaves without brown spots.
- Cauliflower with wrinkled leaves and brown spots should not be picked.
- Celery stalks must be strong and fresh.
- Cucumbers must be hard and have no soft parts whatsoever.
- Withered peas or brown spotted peas should be avoided.
- Fresh peppers with beautiful colors must be picked.
- Spinach leaves must be fresh and free of moisture.

Try to talk to the employees of the general production department. They can let you know when the truck that delivers their goods show up, with a goal to acquire knowledge about delivery of freshest product is on the shelf.

COOKING CONDITIONS AND TECHNIQUES

Success in the kitchen starts with understanding great cooking conditions, the technique and method to prepare fantastic food of restaurant quality.

Most of the ingredients are cut or chopped into small pieces before adding to the recipe. Sometimes the parts have to fit the same size, as well as different sizes on other occasions. Here are the basic cutting techniques.

- Chopping; which means easily cutting ingredients into small pieces. The pieces chopped are normally larger than dices and they do not have to be of uniform sizes. When chopping vegetables, hold the tip of the chef's knife on the chopping board and cut vegetables one at a time with a up and down motion. Pass the ingredients to be chopped through the sharp edge of the knife and keep your fingers bent.

- Dicing means cutting food ingredients into small sizes usually a cube, which is basically ¼–¾ square. When dicing ingredients, set the board and cut the ingredients into the same width as desired. At this point, your Ingredients are set and cut it into cubes shape sizes.

- Mincing is cutting ingredients into very thin slice. When mincing, you usually cut it on a chopping board. Collect pieces in a pile, place your knife on a pile. Keeping the end of contact with the chopping board, continue to lift the sharp edge and lower it by moving the tip in a round segment.

- Grating gives food a very smooth texture and is made possible with a grater.
- Slicing is a method of cutting when you actually cut through ingredients entirely, for example meat, fruit, vegetables, cheese or bread.
- Zesting is a way to remove the peels of the ingredients usually fruits.

Making good use of a knife is an important skill in the kitchen. This is a basic kitchen tool that requires proper care in order to work properly. Try to sharpen the knife with a file, because a blunt knife will slip and you might injure yourself.

There are several ways to prepare meat and vegetables to be cooked. Here are the basics you need to know to make recipes in this book.

- Boiling mean cooking food in boiling water.
- Broiling simply means cooking food under direct heat.
- Deep frying food is involves frying food in large quantity of hot oil until it turns crispy.
- Marinating is done by keeping food in liquid to increase its flavor and make it tender.
- Roasting is a technique which involves cooking food in the oven.

- Stewing means cooking food in liquid in a closed lid pot for a long time until it becomes tender.
- Steaming means cooking food by subjecting it to direct steam or vapor.
- Stir-frying is an Asian technique for cooking small pieces of food quickly in hot oil with constant stirring.

FOOD PRESENTATION

When you go to a restaurant, the presentation at the place becomes as important as the type of food that is served when you decide if you have a satisfying experience. Remember that serving food and setting the table is very useful when serving copycat meals as well. .

GARNISH

The ingredients in a plate can function as a side as well. Store some new chopped herbs needed in a bowl to be taken right before you serve your dish. Use diced tomatoes or onions. Shredded cheese gives a nice touch to almost any dish.

PLATING

There are several types of plating that restaurants use, including:
- Half-and-half dressing style is when the main dish is on one side of the plate and side dishes on the other side.

- The pie style is when the plates are separated by segments of protein, starch and vegetables or other different food classes depending on the servings.
- Family style plating is an arrangement for the family where food is served on large plates aimed at large numbers of people.
- Vertical plating is an arrangement when you place the plate on top, usually with protein on the base while the side dish is placed on top.

DESSERT

To serve a perfectly prepared restaurant dessert, serve it in a unique drinking glass. A small glass of wine with cake, fruit juices and ice cream makes for a pleasant presentation. Sundaes and cakes in shot glasses can no doubt be made for home cooks. It's time to raise your bar and fill the glasses with dessert. Small glasses also work wonderfully when serving snacks that are valued after meals.

CHAPTER 2:

ADVANTAGES OF HOMEMADE

FAST FOOD

In the 1950s and 1960s, fast food restaurants became widespread in many networks. They suggest useful alternatives for organizing all dishes on spot and getting them in a few moments.

Their costs are much better than real restaurants. The food is simple but delicious and provides easy answers for busy families and work experts. It's clear why fast food from restaurants in the United States soon becomes an important business opportunity.

At the same time it turns out to be well known by a wide variety of people. In fact, Sodacraft Andy Warhol even released a short film in which he ate a McDonald's burger to build fast food from restaurants as an inseparable part of American culture. However, a long time passed and we learned fast food products from restaurants that should have made us question our desire for fast food.

We have provided important benefits of homemade food. Ideally, you will be convinced that pre-cooking at home is a much cheaper and more satisfying alternative.

HEALTH CHOICE

It is so guarantee that anything you cook at home is healthier than fast food in restaurants because you are the one in charge.

There are many films and stories that illustrate the unwanted nature of fast food from restaurants. In addition, preparing healthy foods is much easier if you have 100% control over the ingredients used.

As more and more fast food restaurants try to be open to their ingredients and cooking techniques, it is increasingly difficult to keep an eye on everything or to confirm their words in any way.

However, if you cook at home, you can choose whether your dish is deliberately low-fat, sodium-free or completely free of other toxic supplements.

ENHANCING YOUR COOKING SKILL

We all would rather be talented chefs one day. This is a brilliant and useful experience that you must have, and it gives you the opportunity to prepare unusual dishes for your friends, family and guests.

However, many of us often think about inspiration or free time to really focus on improving our cooking skills. However, you should prepare homemade food instead of buying fast food in a restaurant. This gives you many opportunities to improve your skills after a while.

If you don't know much about where to start, reading this book, you will have the opportunity to find some amazing explanations about the basics of cooking and the right combination of techniques.

IT AIDS GROUP COOKING

If you don't live alone or have a family, cooking at home can be a routine activity without much stress. Try eating together, or even set a cooking plan so that you don't have to cook every time.

Everyone can see the modified recipe they want to try to present at parties and gatherings. Cooking together can be fun, broad-minded, and consider various innovative thoughts and strategies that need to be applied.

Regardless of whether everyone helps each other in cooking or not, it is still a smart idea to make sense for everyone who is eating together in the same place at the same time. Fast food restaurants do not offer such opportunities and benefits.

CUSTOMIZATION OF MEALS

If you, your friends, or your family tend to have clear dietary restrictions, then preparing homemade food now is the safest approach to evaluating and eating delicious food.

Restaurants will of course require you to rule out the possibility of adhering to your dietary restrictions, but cooking on your own is an extraordinary opportunity to find recipes that are strategically located away from ingredients that you understand.

There are many means to make special efforts to focus on recipes that do not exclude meat, gluten, sugar, or various ingredients that many people cannot eat.

PROVIDES MORE PROMINENT VARIETIES

Fast food restaurants try to vary their best contributions. Unfortunately, these contributions end up as a non-standard adjustment for the style of food they serve.

Fast food from restaurants such as burgers and fries are mediocre American foods. Tacos holds a small rate fraction in Mexican food as well pizza for Italian foods

HOMEMADE DISHES ARE COST EFFICIENT

Cooking at home is usually far more expensive than fast food from restaurants. While the loneliness of eating at fast food restaurants at that time seemed attractive because of their low value, it is usually possible to prepare comparable meals at home at a modest cost.

Finally, the cost of fast food from restaurants includes the cost of convenience and order. If you prepare detailed home-cooked meals early and buy certain ingredients in large quantities, you can save a lot of money every week.

However, it takes more effort to plan and prepare your own food, but at the end of the process, you will find that stress can be justified in spite of all the problems.

CHAPTER 3:

MCDONALD COPYCAT RECIPES

HAMBURGER SEASONING

Use this spice on all your McDonald's copycat burgers.

Ingredients
- 4 tbsps. of salt
- 2 tbsps. of monosodium glutamate
- 1 tsp. of black pepper
- ¼ tsp. of onion powder

Directions

Mix all ingredients well. Use in a whisk with a hole large enough to make pepper flow in.

This spice is used generously in all McDonald's burgers during the cooking process.

BIG X-TRA SEASONING

Ingredients
- 3 tbsps. of sea salt
- 3 tsps. of spice oil
- 1 square minced meat chunks
- ¼ tsp. dark pepper

Directions

Mix all the ingredients in a bowl and let it cool for a while.

This special seasoning is only used for Big X-Tra.

REGULAR HAMBURGER

Preparation Time: 10 minutes

Cooking Time: 25 minutes

Servings 10

Ingredients
- 10 Hamburger buns
- 10 Beef patties
- 1cup of sliced onion

- Pickles
- Mustard
- Tomato sauce
- Wax paper
- McDonald's hamburger seasoning

Directions

Beef Patties;

Divides 1 pound of meat into 10 equal balls. Create the structure of the patties from each ball is about a diameter of 2 inches and ¼ inches thick. Do this on wax paper.

Currently freezing the patties for 60 minutes just in case. (This prevents them from falling apart when grilling.) Obviously, you will do this before the "burger preparation" time. Make 9 more patties this way.

Onion;

Place the dried onion in the bowl and add water. The water should be several centimeters above the tip of the onion. (It's better to have much water than little.) Cover and put in the refrigerator for about half an hour.

Separate the liquid from the onion. Cover again and cool in fridge until "burger preparation."

Pickles;

Cut the pickles into small thin slices

1. Preheat your oven to warm up - at least to its level, this is for a different time. You will need two electric grills - one for grilling meat and one for baking bread.

2. Preheat meat grill to 375-400 °F and buns grill to around 350 °F (this method will make you cook four each). Note: Before you begin, make sure the integrity of your ingredients is maintained.

3. Slightly toast 4 crown buns (top). Carefully place them face down on the grill. Place the base buns on the grill as well. Then apply pressure on the buns so that it would toast evenly.

4. Place the frozen patties on another grill. After about 20 seconds, "grill" by applying even weight to the back of the metal spatula and pressing the front with your free hand. (Be careful that your fingers don't burn.) This should only be done for about 2 seconds. You have to hear the patties sizzle when you "grill" them. Sprinkle the seasoning generously after grilling the patties.

5. Your buns should be well toast and very much ready. They should have a tan color when they are of the grill.

6. After about a minute of grilling the patties, turn them over to grill the other side. Be careful not to burn sides. Add seasoning to the other side and sprinkle some onions on it.

7. . Now quickly dress the buns (crown or top). Add mustard, squeezing the mustard bottle five times in a way that the mustard comes out half an inch from the edge. Also add ketchup, squeezing the bottle like you did for the mustard. Place the pickles in between.

8. When you are finished dressing the buns, the patties should be ready. (about 1 minute after flipping to the other side) Lift a patty and tilt so that the fat will drain of the surface. Use your free hand to hold and sprinkle onion on top. Place the patty and onions on the side of the dressing crown and top it with a toasted base buns. (Burgers must be upside down)

9. Place the hamburger so it is upside down in the middle of your pre-cut wax paper. Fold the paper firmly over the burger. It should look like a very oval cylinder with two layers open and a burger in the middle. At this time, the topping wrap opens under the bottom of the burger so that it is tightly wrapped.

Q-ING METHOD

Q-ing is a McDonald's technique used to blends flavor mechanically. For example, making use of heat lamp or microwave.

1. Place the covered hamburger in the preheated oven. (Note ... the oven is pre-warmed) Hold it there for about 8-10 minutes. This is an ample opportunity to cook other sets Important note: some ovens are too hot even at low temperatures and this can make your burger dry. If the burgers eventually look dry, do not use the "Q-ing" method

2. The Q-ing alternative strategy is to wrap the sandwich tightly in wax paper, let it sit for 5 minutes, and turn on the microwave for 15 seconds (while still wrapped). This will complete the Q-ing process without too many microwaving it too much.

ARCH DELUXE

Preparation Time: 20 minutes

Servings 1

Arch Deluxe Sauce

- 1 tbsp. of mayonnaise
- ½ tsp. Grey Poupon
- Peppercorn mustard

Ingredients

- 1 burger bun with sesame seeds
- ¼ pound of beef patty
- 1 piece of American cheese
- 1-2 slices of tomatoes
- 1-2 lettuce, finely chopped
- 1 tbsp. of tomato sauce or ketchup
- 1 tbsp. of chopped onions
- Burger seasoning

Directions

1. Mix the mayonnaise and mustard in a small bowl. Store in a safe place. This is a very essential ingredient.

2. Toast the surface of the buns.

3. Cook the patty on a grill sprinkling salt on one side as and hamburger seasoning on the other.

4. Dress your burger in the following order: Special sauce, tomato sauce, onions, lettuce, tomatoes slices and cheese on the crown

5. Place the cooked beef patty in the dressed crown bun and then the toasted base bun

BIG MAC SAUCE

Ingredients
- ¼ cup mayonnaise
- 2 tbsps. of French salad dressing
- ½ tbsp. of HEINZ sweet enjoyment
- ¼ KRAFT Miracle Whip
- 2 tsps. pickle relish
- 1 tsp. of sugar
- 1 tsp. of dried onion
- 1 tsp. of white vinegar
- 1 tsp. of tomato sauce
- ⅛ tsp. of salt

Directions
Mix the ingredients thoroughly in a small bowl. There should be no streaks. Microwave for 25 seconds and stir again. Cover and refrigerate for 1 hour before use. (So the amount of flavor can melt) Make almost 1 cup enough for about 8 big macs.

BIG MAC

Preparation Time: 25 minutes

Servings 1

Ingredients: (each sandwich)

- 1 ordinary bun with sesame
- 1 plain bun
- 2 freshly frozen beef patties
- 2 tbsps. of Big Mac Sauce
- 2 tsps. of dried onion
- 1 slice of American cheese
- 2 slices of pickles
- ¼ cup grated lettuce

Directions

Remove half the crown from a normal bun and keeping the base bun. The cooking strategy for a Big Mac is basically the same as a regular burger, only the toasting method is insignificant. On a Big Mac, toast on the base bun first. Do this with an extra bun. (This will be your central bun)

Cook the two patties on a grill seasoning the sides with salt and seasoning respectively. After toasting the pieces of buns, add 1 tbsp. of big mac sauce to each base buns. Then add ⅛ cup of chopped lettuce for each buns.

Place a small piece of American cheese on top of lettuce of the real base bun. Place two slices of pickles on the salad in an additional base bun or middle bun.

Then afterwards toast the crown (top) bun. After the patties buns are done, place one on top of the two arranged base buns. Place the middle bun on the base bun and place the crown bun on it.

For "Q-ing" ... wrap the finished Big Mac in 12 "x 18" wax paper as follows

1. Place the burger straight on wax paper. Fold the "long" edge over the paper. (Needed after a cylindrical wrap with a burger in it)

2. Overlap the two open covers on the bottom. Wrap firmly but don't press it like a normal burger.

3. Leave on for 5-8 minutes and let the flavors melt and mix

4. Microwave when wrapped, this should take 15 seconds.

FILET-O-FISH

The sauce used for the hamburger in this recipe is tartar sauce.

Preparation Time: 15 minutes

Servings 1

Special Tools

You will need a deep fryer for this. (This applies to every serving recipe. Increase everything needed for each serving.) Fish patties should also be cooked according to packaging instructions.

Filet-o-fish tartar sauce

- ½ Cup of Kraft Miracle Whip
- ¼ cup of vlasic relish
- 2 tbsps. of dried chopped onion

- 2 tsps. half and half
- 1 tsp. of dried parsley
- ½ tsp. concentrated lemon juice
- 10-12 small caper, minced
- ⅛ tsp. of sugar

Mix in a small container, stir well and refrigerate in a tight compartment until used.

Make this tartar sauce far before the Filet-o-Fish burger. (So that the flavors will melt.

Ingredients
- 1 frozen white fish patty
- 1 normal sized buns
- 1 tbsp. of tartar sauce
- ½ slice of American cheese
- Salt
- 1 sheet of 12 "x 12" wax paper (for wrapping).

Directions
Heat the frying pan to 375-400 °F. After heating, cook the fish for 3-5 minutes without thawing until it is well cooked. Remove from the pan and add salt.

Microwave for about 10 seconds until very hot. (Try not to toast it.)

Add about 1 tbsp. of cooled tartar sauce to the crown of your burger. Place the cooked fish fillet on top, place a piece of American cheese on the fish and add the base bun.

Cover with 12 "x 12" sheets of wax paper and heat them in the oven setting for a minimum of 8-10 minutes. Enjoy the incredible fillet-o-fish!

The replacement strategy for "Q-ing" is to wrap the sandwich tightly in wax paper, let it sit for 5 minutes, and let it sit in the microwave for 15 seconds (while still wrapped).

CHAPTER 4:

KFC COPYCAT RECIPES

BBQ BAKED BEANS

Preparation Time: 20 minutes

Servings 4 to 6.

Ingredients

- 2 cans of 15 ounces white kidney beans (with liquid)
- 2 tbsps. of water
- 1 tbsp. of cornstarch
- ½ bowl tomato sauce
- ½ cup of brown sugar
- 2 tbsps. of white vinegar
- 4 tsps. of minced onions
- 2 pieces of cooked grounded bacon
- ½ tsp. of dried mustard
- ¼ tsp. of salted black pepper with garlic powder

Directions

Preheat the oven to 350 °F. Pour all ingredients from the cans of 15-oz beans into a dish. Mix water with cornstarch in a small bowl until the cornstarch breaks. Add the mixture into the beans. Mix the remaining ingredients in the beans and cover the dish.

Heat for an hour and a half or until the sauce thickens. Let the beans stand for 5 to 10 minutes and then remove from the oven before serving.

PORK BBQ SAUCE

Preparation Time: 25 minutes

Servings 1

Ingredients

- 2½ cups of water
- ¼ glass of vinegar
- 1 tbsp. of sugar
- 3 tsps. of pepper
- 2 tbsps. of butter
- 3 tsps. of salt
- ¼ cup of chopped onion
- 1 clove garlic, minced meat

- 1 tsp. red pepper
- 2 tsps. of chili powder
- 1 tsp. of paprika sauce
- 1 tsp. of dried mustard powder
- 3 tbsps. of Worcestershire sauce

Directions

Mix all ingredients in a saucepan. Heat with constant stirring to boiling point. Reduce the heat and let it simmer for 5 minutes.

Let it cool for a while, warm before use. Start by seasoning the meat at the beginning of the cooking process. Season and rotate until pork is 170°F on the meat thermometer (takes about 20 minutes for ribs.)

BUTTERMILK BISCUITS

Preparation Time: 20 minutes

Servings 18

Ingredients

- ½ cup of butter
- ¼ a glass of club soda
- 1 egg (beaten)
- ¾ glass of milk
- 1 tsp. of salt
- 5 cups of biscuits

Directions

Preheat the oven to 840 °F. Mix all ingredients. Plying the ingredients is done by hand by flouring your hand. Create molds of the mixture on wax paper one inch thick. Bake on a lubricating heating plate for 12 minutes or until it is shiny brown, coat it with a soft seal when it comes out of the oven. Make 18 cookies.

COLESLAW

Preparation Time: 2½ hours

Servings 2-12

Ingredients

- 8 cups of finely chopped cabbage (chopped at the head)
- ¼ cup grated carrot (1 medium carrot)
- 2 tbsps. of chopped onion
- ⅓ glass of granulated sugar
- ½ tsp. of salt
- ⅛ tsp. of black pepper
- ¼ glass of milk
- ½ cup mayonnaise

- ¼ glass of buttermilk
- ½ tbsp. of white vinegar
- 2½ tbsps. of lemon juice

Directions

Make sure the cabbage and carrots are cut into small pieces (make sure the pieces are very small). Mix sugar, salt, pepper, milk, mayonnaise, buttermilk, vinegar and lemon, press into a large bowl and stir until smooth. Add cabbage, carrots and onions, stir well. Cover before serving and refrigerate for 2 hours.

CORN MUFFINS

Preparation Time: 25 minutes

Servings 9

Ingredients

- 1 cup of flour
- 1 cup of cornmeal
- ½ cup of sugar
- 1 tbsp. of baking powder
- ½ tsp. of salt
- ½ cup of margarine
- 1 cup of cream
- 1 egg, beaten briefly

Directions

Preheat the oven to 400 °F. Muffins tin should be oiled for 9 muffins.

Mix flour, cornmeal, sugar, baking powder and salt in a large bowl.

Add margarine and mash until soft. In another bowl, mix the cream with eggs and add the flour mixture to the liquid mixture. Fill the tin with a spoon to the brim.

EXTRA CRISPY

Preparation Time: 30 minutes

Servings 6

Ingredients

- 1 whole chicken

For the covering;

- 1 egg, beaten
- 1 cup of milk
- 2 cups of universal flour
- 2½ tsps. of salt
- ¾ tsp. of black pepper
- ¾ tsp. of monosodium glutamate
- ⅛ tsp. of garlic powder

- ⅛ tsp. of baking soda

Directions

Cut the skin and fat from the chicken pieces. In a deep fryer, heat the oil to 350 °F. Add beaten eggs and milk to a medium bowl.

Combine the remaining ingredients (flour, salt, pepper, and monosodium glutamate) in another medium sized bowl.

After the chicken is marinated, transfer each part to the tissue to drain the excess liquid. If you are working with each piece one at a time, dip the eggs and milk first at this time, cover the chicken with a dry flour mixture. At this point, eggs and milk are mixed again and then returned to flour.

Make sure each part is entirely covered with the mixture. Arrange the chicken on a plate or sheet of care until each part is covered.

Fry the chicken in the deep fryer, with each part shortening to heat. Fry half the chicken at once (4 pieces) for 12-15 minutes or until light brown.

You need to make sure that the chicken is partially stirred during frying time so that each part is fried evenly. Evacuate chickens to a rack or sheet to cool for about 5 minutes before eating.

EXTRA CRISPY STRIPS

Preparation Time: 15 minutes

Servings 6

Ingredients

Marinate:

- 4 cups of water
- 1 tbsp. of salt
- ½ tsp. of monosodium glutamate

Covering:

- 1 egg, broken
- 1 cup of milk
- 2 cups flour (universal)
- 2½ tsps. of salt
- ¾ tsp. of black pepper
- ¾ tsp. of monosodium glutamate
- ⅛ tsp. of garlic powder
- ⅛ tsp. of baking powder

Directions

Cut 6 slices of chicken breast into pieces.

Heat the deep fryer, heating the oil to 350 °F. Beat 1 egg and mix with 1 cup of milk. Dip the chicken in the egg and milk mixture.

Prepare you covering by mixing all the ingredients in a bowl. Dip the chicken in the prepared covering.

Fry the chicken in the deep fryer for several minutes until it is light brown and the chicken is afloat. Remove the chicken on the rack and allow to drain and cool for 5 minutes.

KFC GRAVY

Preparation Time: 1 hour

Servings 3

Ingredients

- 1 tbsp. of vegetable oil
- 5 tbsps. of all purpose flour
- 1 can of Campbell chicken broth (add with 1 bowl of water)
- ¼ tsp. of salt
- ⅛ tsp. of monosodium glutamate or flavoring enhancer
- ⅛ tsp. of black pepper

Directions

Make a mix by adding the vegetable shortening to ½ tbsp. of flour in a saucepan on a stove supplying low heat.

Let this mixture heat on the stove for 20-30 minutes, stirring constantly, until it is dark brown. Remove the mixture from the stove and add the remaining ingredients to the pan and stir.

Put the pan back on the stove, set it to medium and bring to a boil. Reduce heat and make it simmer for 15 minutes or until it thickens. Make about 3 cups.

HONEY BARBECUED WINGS

Preparation Time: 30 minutes

Servings 20

Ingredients

- 20 chicken wings with the tips removed
- 2 cups of flour
- 2 eggs
- ⅔ glass of milk
- 1 can of barbecue Sauce
- ¼ cup of honey
- Oil enough for deep frying

Directions

Wash the chicken wings and remove the wing tips immediately. Slice the other two pieces in half.

Remove water from the wings by shaking. Add eggs and milk to a bowl and stir well. Set in a safe place.

Combine BBQ sauce and honey. Set in a safe place. Place the flour in a bowl and put the wings at this point to cover it gently. Roll the wings in the egg wash and throw them back into the bowl of flower. You need really good coating of flour for the barbecue sauce to hold it together. Repeat 2-3 more times.

Heat a large frying pan. Heat the oil (around 350 °F).

Fry and make sure the wings are light brown. Drain in well in a paper towels

Preheat your oven to 325 °F.

Dip each wing in a barbecue sauce and place it on a greased sheet. Make sure the wings are not connected. Let it cook for 15-20 minutes until it doesn't look shiny anymore.

MACARONI AND CHEESE

Preparation Time: 20 minutes

Servings 6

Ingredients

- 6 cups of water
- ⅓ cup of macaroni
- 4 ounces of cheese (Velveeta)
- ½ cup of cheddar cheese, grated
- 2 tbsps. of pure milk
- ¼ tsp. of salt

Directions

Heat water in a medium saucepan over high heat until it boils. Add the macaroni to the water and cook for 10 to 12 minutes or until it is soft, stirring frequently.

When the macaroni is being cooked, add the cheese sauce and put the remaining ingredients in a small pan over low heat. Stir as often as possible until the cheese has a smooth consistency.

After the macaroni are well cooked, pour and empty it into a similar pan without water. Mix the cheese sauce with the macaroni in the pan and stir gently until the macaroni is coated with cheese. Serve hot.

MACARONI SALAD

Preparation Time: 2½ hours

Servings 1

Ingredients

- 1 pound of macaroni
- ¼ cup of carrot, finely chopped
- 1 tbsp. of chopped onion
- ¼ cup of celery, finely chopped
- 2 glasses of coleslaw dressing

Directions

Boil the macaroni following the directions on the wrapper. Turn off the stove, drain and let it cool.

Mix all of the above Ingredients in a large bowl. Refrigerator for 2 hours.

MASHED POTATOES

Preparation Time: 10 minutes

Servings 6

Ingredients

- 2½ cups of potato flakes
- 1 stick of margarine
- 2 tbsps. of butter
- 2½ glasses of hot water
- ¾ cup of milk
- 1 tsp. of salt

Directions

Boil the water and add the margarine and butter until they soften and melt. Add salt and let it cook for 2 minutes.

Mix the potato flakes with the above mixture and stir until it looks like a regular potato. Add enough milk until the mixture is consistent. Serve 6 with gravy.

CHAPTER 5:

TACO BELL COPYCAT RECIPES

CHEESY BEAN AND RICE BURRITO

Preparation time is 25 minutes

8 servings

Ingredients

- 1½ cup of water
- 1½ cup of raw brown rice
- 1 diced medium green pepper
- ½ cup of chopped onion

- 1 tbsp. of olive oil
- 1 tsp. of chopped garlic
- 1 tbsp. of bean stew powder
- 1 tsp. of ground cumin
- ⅛ tsp. of red pepper powder
- 1 can (15 ounces) of black and red baked beans
- 8 flour tortillas (8 inches), warmed
- 1 cup of salsa
- Optional side garnish: grated cheese with low fat content and low fat sour cream

Directions

Heat the water to boiling point in a small pot. Pour the rice into the boiling water. Allow to cook until it is dark brown; cover and allow to boil for 5 more minutes. Turn off the heat. Let stand for 5 minutes and drain the water.

Meanwhile, fry the green peppers and onions in a large pan for 3-4 minutes in oil until it is tender. Add garlic; cook a little longer. Add the red and black beans, cumin and pepper. Add beans and rice; cook and stir for 4-6 minutes.

Spoon about ½ cup each to fill the tortilla; Add 2 tbsps. of salsa. Fold the sides and the top edge of the tortilla and move it. Mix with cheese and cream.

Nutrient content

1: 290 calories each, 6 g fat (1 g wet fat), 0 cholesterol, 504 mg sodium, 49 g starch (2 g sugar, 4 g fiber), 9 g protein.

NACHO FRIES

Preparation Time: 20 minutes

8 servings

Ingredients
- 1 package (28 ounces) of frozen French fries
- 1 can (10 ounces) of thick, pure cheese soup
- ¼ glass of 2% milk mix
- ½ tsp. of garlic powder
- ¼ tsp. of onion powder
- Paprika

Directions

Arrange the French fries in separate layers with 2 ways 15x10x1-in baking sheet. Cook for 15-18 minutes at 450 °F or until it is golden brown, soft and shiny.

Mix soup, milk, garlic powder and onion powder in a small saucepan. Heat thoroughly. Then spread on the French fries; Sprinkle with paprika

Nutrient content

1 serving: 166 calories, 5 g fat (2 g dipped fat), 2 mg cholesterol, 657 mg sodium, 27 g starch (3 g sugar, 3 g fiber), 3 g protein.

DRESSED EGG TACO

Preparation Time: 25 minutes

8 servings

Ingredients

- ⅓ cup of dark beans, washed and drained
- A cup of diced avocados
- ½ a glass of Pico de Gallo
- 1 tbsp. of lime juice
- 1 cup of frozen potatoes, thawed
- ½ pound of pork sausage
- 6 large eggs
- 2 tbsps. of 2% milk

- ½ cup grated Monterey Jack cheese
- 8 flour tortillas (6 inches), warmed
- Sour cream, optional
- Cilantro freshly cut, optional
- Extra Pico de Gallo, optional

Directions

Carefully mix the black beans, avocado, pico de galo and lime juice. Keep it in a safe place. Boil potatoes in a large pot or other saucepan and mash the sausage over medium-high heat until it is very hot. Cook for 6-8 minutes until the point where the sausage is pink and potatoes tender.

Beat eggs and mix together with milk. Pour in the pan; cook and stir over medium heat until the eggs thicken and no liquid mix remains. Add the cheese. Fill the eggs mix in tortillas with a spoon; Top with black bean mixture. Whenever you want, add a large cream, cilantro and extra pico de galo.

Nutrient content

1 taco: 291 calories, 16 g fat (6 g wet fat), 161 mg cholesterol, 494 mg sodium, 22 g starch (1 g sugar, 3 g fiber), 13 g protein.

CHEESE QUESADILLA

Preparation Time: 15 minutes

6 servings

Ingredients
- 4 flour tortillas (8 inches), warmed
- 1 cup of grated Mexican cheese mixture
- ½ cup of salsa

Directions
Place tortillas on a baking sheet. Combining cheese and salsa; cover each slice of tortilla and fold.
Put the stove on each side for 3 minutes or until it is shiny brown. Cut into wedges.

Nutrient content

1 serving: 223 calories, 11 g fat (5 g dyed fat), 25 mg cholesterol, 406 mg sodium, 21 g starch (1 g sugar, 1 g fiber), 9 g protein.

CHICKEN BURRITO

Preparation time: 20 minutes
Cooking time: 35 minutes.
Servings: 2 curries (6 servings each)

Ingredients

- 6 tbsps. of margarine
- 1 large onion, finely chopped
- ¼ cup of chopped peppers
- ½ cup of all purpose flour
- 3 cups of chicken broth
- 1 can (10 ounces) diced tomatoes and green chilies
- 1 tsp. of ground cumin

- 1 tsp. of bean powder soup
- ½ tsp. of garlic powder
- ½ tsp. of salt
- 2 tbsps. of chopped black pepper, optional
- 1 can (15 ounces) boiled with beans
- 1 pack (8 ounces.) Cream cheese, diced
- 8 cups diced boiled chicken
- 24 flour tortillas (6 inches), warmed
- 6 cups of shredded Monterey Jack cheese
- Salsa, optional

Directions

Preheat the oven to 350 °F. Heat the margarine over medium heat in a pan. Add onions and pepper; cook and stir until soft. Mix flour until everything it blends well. Add broth step by step. Heat to boiling point and stir for 2 minutes till it turns dark brown; Mix with tomatoes and spice. Leave on for 5 minutes. Add soup and cream cheese; Stir until the cream cheese is softened, then add chicken.

Place about half a cup of filling in the middle of each tortilla; Sprinkle each with a cup of Colby Monterey Jack cheese. Fold the base and sides above the surface and move off. Fill in 2 13x9 inches of oiled baking sheet.

Cook for 35-40 minutes or until it is warm. Whenever you want, serve with salsa.

Nutrient content

2 burritos: 760 calories, 44 g fat (23 g dipped fat), cholesterol 177 mg, 1608 mg sodium, 40 g starch (2 g sugar, 2 g fiber), 51 g protein.

GUACAMOLE SIDE

Preparation Time: 10 minutes

2 servings

Ingredients
- 3 medium-sized avocados, peeled and sliced
- 1 clove garlic, minced meat
- ¼ to ½ tsp. of salt
- 2 medium tomatoes, and chopped, optional
- 1 small onion, finely chopped
- ¼ cup mayonnaise, optional
- 1 to 2 tbsps. of lime juice
- 1 tbsp. of minced cilantro

Directions

Mix mashed avocado with garlic and salt in a bowl. Mix other ingredients with the mixture. Avocados contain monounsaturated fat, a decent fat which can lower your blood cholesterol, along with the risk of stroke and heart disease.

Add other tasty garnish to your dish to add more taste and flavor.

In this recipe, you can use an alternative for lemon and lime juice to get an alternative flavor. However, to replace oranges, you need to use a little lemon or lime to enhance the flavors.

Nutrient content

¼ glass: 90 calories, 8 g fat (1 g fat dipped), 0 cholesterol, 78 mg sodium, 6 g starch (1 g sugar, 4 g fiber), 1 g protein. Diabetes metabolism: 1½ fat.

SPICY TOSTADA

Preparation Time: 30 minutes

4 servings

Ingredients
- ½ pound of ground beef (90% lean)
- 1 can (10 ounces) diced moisturized tomatoes and green chilies
- 1 can (15 ounces) of black and red beans washed and drained
- 1 can (16 ounces) of cooked processed beans
- 8 shells of tostada

Optional garnish: mix of low-fat Mexican cheese, chopped lettuce, salsa and sour cream

Directions

In a large pot, cook the ground beef over medium heat and cook for 4-6 minutes until it turns pink. Mix the tomatoes; heat it to boiling point. Reduce heat; and make it stew for 6-8 minutes until the liquid is almost gone. Mix the black beans; Heat thoroughly.

Serve the beans on a tostada shell and top with the ground beef mixture; Add all other ingredients to the tostada shell.

Nutrient content

2 tostada 392 calories, 14 g fat (4 g dipped fat), 35 mg cholesterol, 1011 mg sodium, 46 g starch (2 g sugar, 10 g fiber), 23 g protein.

FIESTA TACO SALAD

Preparation Time: 25 minutes

8 servings (1 cup sauce)

Ingredients

- 1 lb. of ground meat
- ½ cups of taco seasoning, divided
- 1 medium chopped iced lettuce,
- 1 can (16 ounces) kidney beans, washed and drain water
- 1 large onion, finely chopped

- 4 medium sized tomatoes, finely chopped with the seeds removed
- 2 cups shredded cheddar cheese
- 4 cups of grated tortilla chips (about 8 ounces)
- 1 container (8 ounces) salad dressing
- 2 tbsps. of taco sauce

Directions

Cook the meat in a large pot over medium heat and cook for 6-8 minutes until it turns pink. Remove from the pot and mix 3 tbsps. of taco seasoning.

Line the meat, lettuce, beans, onions, tomatoes, cheese and chopped chips in a large bowl. In another small bowl, mix the garnish with the remaining salad dressing, taco sauce and taco sauce. Serve the with the taco salads.

Nutrient content

1 cup of salad with 2 tbsps. of sauce: 574 calories, 34 g fat (11 g wet fat), 66 mg cholesterol, 1109 mg sodium, 44 g starch (9 g sugar, 5 g fiber), 23 g protein.

GRANDE SCRAMBLER

Preparation Time: 30 minutes

Servings: 12 burritos

Ingredients

- 1 pound of pork sausage
- 1½ cup frozen brown potatoes, diced
- ¼ cup of chopped onion
- ¼ cup diced green or red chili
- 4 large eggs, beaten smoothly
- 12 flour tortillas (8 inches), warmed
- ½ cup grated cheddar cheese
- Optional: Picante sauce and sour cream

Directions

Cook the pot sausage in a large pot over medium heat until they turn pink. Then includes potatoes, onions, and black pepper; cook and stir for 6-8 minutes or until tender. Including eggs; cook and stir until it is well cooked.

Fill each tortilla with a spoonful of the mixture prepared above. Sprinkle some cheese on it. Cover the sides and surface above with the tortilla. Serve with hot picante sauce and hot cream whenever you want.

To Freeze And Heat A Tortilla: Wrap each tortilla in wax paper and tinfoil. Freeze for a while. Remove the foil and wax paper to make use of the tortilla. Place tortilla on a plate and heat in a microwave. Microwave on high heat for 2 to 3 minutes or until the thermometer reaches about 165 °F, flip the tortilla and put back into the microwave for 20 seconds.

Nutrient content

1 tortilla: 303 calories, 15 g fat (5 g wet fat), 87 mg cholesterol, 521 mg sodium, 30 g starch (0 sugar, 2 g fiber), 12 g protein.

CHICKEN QUESADILLA

Preparation Time: 30 minutes

6 servings

Ingredients

- 2½ cups of shredded boiled chicken
- ⅔ glass of salsa
- ⅓ Grind a slice of onion
- ¾ to 1 tsp. of ground cumin
- ½ tsp. of salt
- ½ tsp. of dried oregano
- 6 flour tortillas (8 inches)

- 2 cups shredded cheddar cheese
- Guacamole and sour cream

Directions

Mix the first 6 ingredients in a large saucepan. Cook without covering over medium heat for about 10 minutes, stirring consistently.

Spread 1 side of the tortillas with margarine; Place the spread side on a finely folded baking sheet. Spoon ⅓ cup of chicken mixture from each tortilla; Sprinkle 1 tbsp. of cheese on the tortilla.

Cover the smooth side of the tortilla with cheese. Heat at 375 °F for 9-11 minutes until they are fresh and shiny brown. Cut into slices and serve with sour cream and guacamole.

Tips

Boneless chicken skin works very well in a medium oven. The meat is shredded efficiently, but it remains moist because of its slightly higher fat content.

Nutrient content

Every 1: 477 calories, 26 g fat (13 g wet fat), 106 mg cholesterol, 901 mg sodium, 27 g starch (1 g sugar, 1 g fiber), 31 g protein.

CHAPTER 6:

IKEA COPYCAT RECIPES

YELLOW PEAS HUMMUS WITH KIMCHI OIL

Preparation Time: 4 hours
Serves 4-6

Ingredients
Hummus:
- 2½ cups of dried yellow peas
- 2-3 cloves of garlic
- 3 tbsps. of light tahini
- ½ tsp. of ground cumin
- 4–5 tbsp. lemon juice to add flavor
- 2 tbsps. of turnip oil
- Salt to improve taste

- 1 cup of boiling water
- ½ cup hot onion, finely chopped

Kimchi Oil:
- 1½ cup of turnip oil
- ½ cup of vinegar
- ½ - 1 tsp. bean stew powder to add flavor
- 1 small garlic clove, finely chopped
- 1 tsp. of ginger, finely chopped
- 1 tsp. of fish sauce
- ½ -1 tsp. of lime juice

Directions

Place the yellow peas in a bowl with 5 cups of water and let it absorb the moisture for about 1 hour

Drain the peas, rinse and place in a medium-sized saucepan with 3½ cups water and 1 tsp. of salt. Heat to a boiling point, then lower the temperature and let it simmer for 1½-2 hours. Remove the foam that initially rise to the surface.

However, pour about 1 cup of boiled water.

Set aside 1¼ cup of cooked peas. Add the remaining cooked peas together with the remaining ingredients, half a glass of boiled water and 1 tsp. of salt, then process in a blender.

Stir for a few moments. Add more water or salt whenever you want. Mix with some turnip oil and stir for 1 minute.

Heat 1 tbsp. of oil in a large pan. Toast the remaining fresh peas and season with salt. Let it cool and mix with kimchi oil.

Serve peas with kimchi butter on a plate and 2 tbsps. of hummus. Sprinkle a little extra kimchi oil. Sprinkle with finely chopped chives.

SALMON RILLETTES

Preparation Time: 45 minutes

Servings 8

Ingredients

- 0.9lb of hot smoked salmon
- 4 onions
- 1 tbsp. of turnip oil with margarine
- 2 tbsps. garlic garnish
- 1 cup of jalapeño pepper
- Salty chips
- 4 loaves of bread
- Pickles
- ½ cup of lemon juice
- 2 tsps. of sugar

- 1- 1½ cup water
- 1 tsp. salt for the pickles
- Sour cream

Seasoning:
- 3 dark peppercorn
- 1 tsp. of coriander seeds
- 1 large cucumber, cut into pieces
- ½ cup fresh dill chopped
- 1 cup of turnip, cut the slices in the middle
- 1 cup of radish
- 1 cup of yellow beets
- ½ cup of freshly chopped herbs
- 7 tbsps. of turnip oil
- ⅓ cup of cauliflower, sliced
- ⅓ cup of pickles, cut into pieces
- ¼ cup of onion, sliced
- 1 cup of stuffed coriander leaves

Directions

Pickles:

Heat the vinegar, sugar and water, then light the flavor. Stir until the sugar has dissolved and add the sliced pickles.

Cucumbers and dill

Add 1 tsp. of salt after the sugar has broken down. Let it cool before pouring it over the sliced cucumbers on a perfect plate.

Let it marinate for 60 minutes. Place in a bowl and mix with chopped dill.

Radish:
Wash radishes and cut the roots before using.
Put it in the medium bowl. Pour the marinade over the radishes and leave to infuse for 8 minutes at any time before serving.
Serve in a bowl with 2 tbsps. of sour cream and 2 tbsps. of turnip oil.

Yellow Beet:
Heat the beet gently in mild salt water.
Pour in the water and let the beets cool before peeling and chopping.
Place it in a medium bowl and pour it over the cucumber mix.
Allow to cool 12 minutes before serving.
Put the beets in a bowl. Combine with 2 tbsps. of sour cream and 2 tbsps. of turnip oil.
Sprinkle with freshly chopped herbs.

Coriander mix
Place the coriander in the perfect bowl. Pour the pickled liquid and let it infuse for 8 minutes and allow to cool before serving.
Serve in a bowl with 2 tbsps. of sour cream and 2 tbsps. of turnip oil.

Salmon rillettes

Cut the salmon into small pieces with a fork in a bowl.

Finely chop the onions and fry gently in 1 tbsp. of turnip oil with a seasoning until it well fried and crispy.

Cut most of the jalapeño and mix with the lemon juice.

Mix some onions, jalapeño and some salt with salmon. Mix 2 tbsps. of turnip oil with wild garlic and season with salt.

Transfer the rillettes to a container with the lid tightly closed, if it is not served immediately cool for about 10 minutes

Cut the salted cucumber and cut the jalapeño smoothly and mixed them together.

For the bread

Apply turnip oil on both sides of the bread. Toast in a pan until its shiny, about 1 minute for each side and sprinkle a pinch of salt.

Serve salmon rolls in a plate with toast and cucumbers.

CUCUMBER SERVING OF SALAD WITH LEMON ZEST, DILL AND SESAME SEEDS

Preparation Time: 5 minutes

Servings 4

Ingredients

- 2 cucumbers, long and thinly sliced
- 1½ cup of fresh dill
- 1 cup of lemon zest
- 2 tbsps. of white sesame seeds, roasted

- 2 tbsps. of salt-flavored radish oil and dill-flavored pepper for additional flavor (optional)

Directions

Place the cucumber on a serving plate.

Mix with dill, lemon zest and sesame.

Pour a spoon of turnip oil and season with salt and pepper.

Sprinkle with some dill (and turnip) and serve immediately.

NETTLE AND WILD GARLIC SOUP WITH POTATOES & ONIONS

Preparation Time: 15 minutes

Servings 4

Ingredients

- 2 onions, sliced
- 1 large garlic clove
- 2 potatoes, finely diced
- 1¼ cup of bramble
- ½ cup of wild garlic (add flowers if you have them)
- 3½ cups of good quality vegetable broth

- 1½ glass of dry white wine
- 1 + 2 tbsps. of turnip oil with margarine flavor
- Radish oil with wild garlic flavor for garnish
- A ½ slice of lemon juice
- 2 tbsps. of dried wild garlic buds
- Salt and pepper for seasoning (Optional)

Directions

To one of the onions, finely dice. Cut the others into fine slices. Heat 1 tbsp. of turnip oil with the seasoning for flavor in a large pot. Then add the onions, garlic and diced potatoes and a pinch of salt.

Cook with medium heat for 5-10 minutes until it soften.

In another small pot pour the onion slices in 2 tbsps. of turnip oil and a pinch of salt over low heat, stirring occasionally.

Add wine to the mixture of onions, garlic and potatoes, then allow to cook for 5 minutes.

Pour into broth and simmer for 10 minutes.

Meanwhile, boil 1 cup water with a little salt.

Add the diced potato and simmer briefly until tender. Remove the potatoes carefully and allow them to drain in a colander.

Add the brambles and blend with the mix. At this point, add the wild garlic leaves and boil for 2 minutes.

Remove from the stove and process in a blender.

Season with salt and pepper, if necessary, and lemon juice

Fill a plate with the bramble mix and top with diced potatoes, fine chopped onions, buds and flowers of wild garlic if available.

Sizzle with some radish oil and wild garlic powder and serve it with bread and butter with sea salt as preferred.

GRILLED VEGGIES WITH FRIED WHOLE GRAIN MIX AND BROTH

Preparation Time: 25 minutes

Servings 1

Ingredients

1 large zucchini, cut into lumps

8 small carrots, cut into pieces

2 eggplants

Lots of turnips, sliced

1 large lemon, slices

1½ cup whole wheat mix, cooked

3 tbsps. of turnip oil

3 tbsps. ofthyme flavor

1 cup of high-quality, warm vegetable broth

Directions

Fry whole wheat mixture in 1 tbsp. of turnip oil.

Drain in a paper towel. Store and allow to cool in a safe place.

Carefully spread all vegetables adding a few drops of turnip oil to cover it gently.

Sprinkle the surface with salt and pepper.

Cut the eggplants with a fork.

Heat the grill over medium heat and start with the eggplant.

Cook it gently until it falls apart. At this point, you find that they are ready and soft inside. Place it on a chopping board on a tinfoil

Heat the oven to high heat.

Place the remaining vegetables and cook until soft and tender and they are seared everywhere.

Cut eggplants into equal parts.

Place all the vegetables on a serving plate and season with a few drops of sliced lemon and sprinkle some salt and pepper.

Mix the warm vegetable broth and whole grains together

Sprinkle with thyme flavor and turnip oil and serve immediately.

GRILLED VEGETABLES WITH BURRATA AND TURNIP OIL

Preparation Time: 15 minutes

Servings 1

Ingredients

- 2 cups of washed peas
- 4 onions, finely sliced
- 4 jalapeños
- Salt and pepper for flavor

- 2 packs of fresh burrata balls
- Lots of fresh green herbs
- 1 cup of turnip oil
- Lemon juice
- Large breads for serving

Directions

Bleach the herb stems in boiling water for 10 seconds

Drain and stir in a blender with turnip oil until it smoothen into a puree

Place a colander under a bowl and apply pressure to empty the whole puree into the drain. Leave it for a minute for it to drain entirely.

Season with a few drops of lemon juice and a pinch of salt.

Carefully spread all vegetables in a few drops of turnip oil to cover it gently.

Sprinkle with salt and pepper.

Heat the oven on medium to high heat.

Carefully place the vegetables on the oven and cook until they are soft, tender and seared entirely.

Remove from the oven and chop some jalapeños into the mixture.

Put all the vegetables in a bowl.

Place the burrata ball on top and pour it with turnip oil and herbs.

GRILLED LITTLE GEM LETTUCE WITH TURNIP MAYONNAISE AND CHIMICHURRI

Preparation Time: 30 minutes

Servings 4

Ingredients

Green Salad:

- 4 lettuce each sliced into half
- 2 tbsps. of turnip oil
- Sea salt and pepper for the seasoning
- 2 tbsps. of fresh dill

Turnip Mayonnaise:

- 2 egg yolks
- 1 tbsp. Dijon mustard
- 2½ cups of natural turnip oil
- 1 tbsp. of lemon juice
- 1 tbsp. of vinegar
- Salt for seasoning

Chimichurri:

- 1 cup red wine vinegar
- 1 tsp. of table salt for seasoning
- 2 cloves of garlic, minced
- 1 small onion, finely chopped
- 1 green jalapeño, finely chopped
- ½ cup of freshly cilantro
- ½ cup of fresh parsley, chopped
- 2 tbsps. of Oregano, finely chopped
- 2 tbsps. of garlic, finely chopped
- 1 cup of radish oil with dill flavor

Directions

Mayonnaise:

Beat the egg yolks, vinegar and mustard together.

Slowly turn over most of the butter and stir it constantly until it thickens.

Add the lemon juice and add the remaining turnip oil while stirring vigorously.

Season with salt and store in an airtight container.

Chimichurri:

Mix vinegar, salt, garlic, onion and jalapeño. Leave for 10 minutes.

Mix cilantro, parsley, oregano and garlic.

Use a fork to spread turnip oil on the mixture.

Heat a frying pan or saucepan on medium heat and add some turnip oil to heat.

Stir the lettuce until soft on the outside and tender inside, for about 2 minutes per side.

Place it on a serving plate and season with sea salt and dark pepper.

Serve with mayonnaise, turnip oil, chimichuri and some fresh dill.

CHAPTER 7:

CHEESE CAKE FACTORY AND CHICK-FIL-A COPYCAT RECIPE

CHEESECAKE FACTORY COPYCAT RECIPES
THE CHEESECAKE FACTORY'S TUNA TATAKI SALAD

Servings 4

Preparation Time: 10 minutes

Cooking time: 5 minutes

Ingredients

For tuna:

- 1 pound of tuna, sashimi
- 4 tbsps. of avocado oil

For salads:

- 4 radishes, peeled and finely chopped
- 8 cups of lettuce
- 4 onions, finely chopped
- 4 avocados, peeled, cut roots
- 2 tsps. black sesame

For salad dressing:

- 2 pieces of 1 inch ginger, grate
- 2 tbsps. of liquid stevia
- 4 tbsps. of ponzu sauce, low in carbohydrates
- 2 tbsps. of wine
- 2 tbsps. of soy sauce
- 2 tbsps. of toasted sesame oil

Directions

Prepare the salad dressing by taking a jar, pouring all the ingredients into it, closing the lid and stirring until evenly mixed. Set aside until needed.

To a large salad bowl, add the avocado slices, radishes and lettuce in it and stir until mixed.

Prepare tuna by taking a large pot, put it on medium heat, add oil and when it is hot add tuna and then cook on the side for 1 minute until it is brown.

Place the tuna on a plate, repeat with the remaining tuna, let it cool for 15 minutes and then cut the tuna into thin slices.

Spread the salad evenly on four plates, add the sliced tuna and coat it with the prepared salad dressing.
Sprinkle with sesame and onions on the tuna and serve.

Nutritional information
594 Cal; 42.2 g fat; 37.1 g protein; 4.4 g of net carbohydrates; 12 g of fiber;

LAVA CAKE

Servings 4

Preparation Time: 10 minutes

Cooking time: 12 minutes

Ingredients

- 8 tbsps. of cocoa powder
- 1 tsp. of baking soda
- 2 tsps. of vanilla extract,
- 6 tbsps. of erythritol sweetener
- 6 tbsps. of heavy whipped cream
- 4 eggs

Directions

Pre-heat the oven, set it to 350°F and let it heat up first.

Meanwhile, take four cake molds, coat them with butter, and set aside until you need them.

In a medium bowl, add cocoa powder, add baking soda and erythritol and stir until everything is mixed.

In a separate medium bowl, break some eggs in it, whisk with a fork, then whip the vanilla and cream until mixed.

Beat the egg mixture in the cocoa mixture until everything is smooth, then pour one spoonful of the mixture between the four molds for the cake and then bake for 12 minutes until the top of each set of cakes is still moist.

When it is well baked, turn each mold on a serving plate and serve them.

Nutritional information

192 cal; 15 g fat; 9 g protein; 4 g of carbohydrates; 4 g fiber;

GARLIC CHEDDAR BISCUITS

Servings 12

Preparation Time: 10 minutes

Cooking time: 15 minutes

Ingredients

- ⅓ cup of coconut flour
- 1 tsp. of chopped garlic
- ¼ tsp. of salt
- 2 tbsps. of sour cream
- ¼ tsp. of baking powder
- 1¼ tsp. of seasoning
- 4½ tbsps. of butter melted, cooled and without salt
- 1½ cup of grated cheese
- 4 eggs

Directions

Preheat the oven, set it to 400 °F and let it heat up first.

Then take a large bowl, put the butter in it, add salt, cream and eggs and stir until smooth.

Mix garlic, baking powder, herbs and seasoning until mixed, then fold the cheese until evenly mixed.

Take muffin cans with 12 cups, coat with oil and then fill each cup with the mixture prepared.

The biscuits should be baked for 15 minutes or more until the top is golden brown.

When well baked, let the biscuits cool in the pan for 10 minutes, then serve.

Nutritional information

135 Cal; 11 g fat; 5 g protein; 1 g net carbohydrates; 1 g of fiber;

CHICK-FIL-A COPYCAT RECIPES
CHICK-FIL-A FROZEN LEMONADE

Servings 2

Preparation Time: 5 minutes;

Ingredients

- 1 pack mixture of lemonade, without sugar
- 2 cups of vanilla ice cream, no sugar
- ¼ glass of lemon juice
- 1 glass of water

Directions

Place all ingredients in the order listed above (except ice cream) in the food processor, cover and then blend for 10 seconds until everything is smooth.

Add ice cream and continue mixing for 10 seconds until the drink has the desired consistency.

Put the lemonade into two glasses and serve.

Nutritional information

546 Cal; 45.5 g fat; 5.5 g protein; 28 g of carbohydrates; 5.5 g of fiber;

CHICK-FIL-A SAUCE

Servings 4

Preparation Time: 5 minutes;

Ingredients

- ¼ tsp. of onion powder
- ¼ tsp. of garlic salt
- ½ tbsp. of yellow mustard
- ¼ tsp. of smoked red pepper
- ½ tbsp. of stevia extract powder
- 1 tsp. of liquid smoke
- ½ cup mayonnaise

Directions

Add all the ingredients in a food processor, cover with a lid, and then pulse for 30 seconds until evenly blend.

Pour the sauce in a bowl and serve.

Nutritional information

183 Cal; 20 g of fat; 0 g protein; 0 g without carbohydrates; 0 g of fiber;

BURGER SAUCE

Servings 12

Preparation Time: 5 minutes;

Ingredients

- 1 tbsp. of chopped pickles
- ½ tsp. chopped dill
- ¾ tsp. of onion powder
- ¾ tsp. of garlic powder
- ⅛ tsp. white pepper
- 1 tsp. mustard powder
- ½ tsp. erythritol sweetener
- ¼ tsp. of paprika
- 1 tsp. of white vinegar
- ½ cup mayonnaise

Directions

In a medium bowl, add all ingredients of the sauce and stir well.

Place the sauce in the refrigerator for at least one night to develop the flavor, then serve with a burger.

Nutritional information

15 cal; 7 g fat; 0 g protein; 0 g without carbohydrates; 0 g of fiber; ingredients

POLLO TROPICAL'S CURRY MUSTARD SAUCE

Servings 12

Preparation Time: 5 minutes;

Ingredients

- 2 tsps. of curry powder
- 4 tsps. of mustard paste
- 8 tbsps. of mayonnaise

Directions

Turn on the food processor, add all the ingredients, cover with a lid, and then pulse for 30 seconds until smooth and evenly mixed

Pour the sauce in a bowl and serve.

Nutritional information

66 Cal; 7 g fat; 1 g protein; 0 g without carbohydrates; 1 g of fiber; ingredients

EL FENIX CHILI SAUCE

Servings 28

Preparation Time: 5 minutes

Cooking time: 40 minutes

Ingredients

- 2 tbsps. of coconut flour
- ½ tsp. of salt
- ½ tsp. of black pepper
- ½ tsp. of dried oregano leaf
- 1½ tsp. of garlic powder
- 2 tsps. of cumin
- ½ tsp. of coriander
- 2 tbsps. of oatmeal
- 2 tbsps. of red chili powder
- ⅛ tsp. of dried thyme leaves
- ½ cup of lard
- 2 cups of beef broth

Directions

In a medium-sized saucepan, place on a stove with medium heat, add lard and stir in the flour for 3 to 5 minutes after it has melted until it turns brown. Remove the pan from the stove to cool slightly and then return to the fire.

Mix oatmeal, garlic, thyme, oregano, cumin and coriander, then cook with constant stirring for 2 minutes until it thickens. Then stir the broth until it is even and smooth, set the stove to low and let the sauce boil for 30 minutes until the sauce thickens.

Remove the pan from the stove and then serve.

Nutritional information

22 cal; 2 g of fat; 0 g protein; 0 g without carbohydrates; 0 g of fiber; ingredients

CHAPTER 8:

STARBUCKS COPYCAT RECIPES

PETITE VANILLA BEAN SCONES

Preparation Time: 45 minutes

Servings 8

Ingredients

For the scones

- 2½ cup of flour
- 6 tbsps. of sugar
- 1 tbsp. of baking powder
- ¼ tsp. of salt

- ½ tsp. of cubed butter
- ½ cups of cream (heavy)
- 1 egg
- ½ cup of scraped vanilla beans
- 2 tsp. of extract of vanilla

For the Glaze
- 2 cups of powdered sugar
- 1 tsp. extract of vanilla
- ½ cup of scraped vanilla beans
- 6 tbsp. of cream (heavy)

Directions

Preheat the oven to 400 °F.

Line the baking sheet with the ingredients or aluminum heating sheet.

Mix flour, sugar, baking powder, and salt.

Pulses and stir to mix ingredients

Add some butter and pulse until it is mixed and has a surface like corn flour mix.

In a bowl, stir the cream, eggs, and vanilla extract and beans.

Mix wet and dry ingredients and stir until a smooth mixture is obtained.

Put the mixture to the floured surface and knead the mixture 4-5 times until it sticks together.

Roll the mixture as a whole and with an 8x10 "square shape, about 1" thick.

Cut the dough in half along the long path at this point and make four small square shapes.

At this point, cut each one from corner to corner and make 8 cones

Place the cones on a neat baking sheet and bake for 14 to 18 minutes or until it is golden brown and stick toothpicks through them to remove them easily.

Place it on a rack to cool

Mix the glaze ingredients gradually mixing 1 tbsp. of cream until the desired thickness is achieved.

After the cones have cooled, apply a good coating to each and let it harden for 10 minutes before serving.

PUMPKIN LATTE

Preparation Time: 25 minutes

Serve 1

Ingredients

For the syrup

- ½ cup of water
- ½ cup of sugar
- ⅓ glass of pumpkin puree
- ½ tsp. of cinnamon
- 1 tsp. of nutmeg
- ½ tsp. of cloves
- ½ tsp. of ginger

For the latte

- 8 glasses of milk
- 4 cups of strong coffee or espresso
- 2 tbsps. of pumpkin syrup
- 5 cups of whipped cream
- Pumpkin pie seasoning

Directions

Boil some water and sugar in a saucepan over medium heat and stir until the sugar mix with the ingredients.

Add the seasoning and pumpkin and allow to simmer for 10 minutes, stirring constantly.

Discard heat and pressure through cheesecloth or filter.

Let the syrup cool and at this point cool it in an airtight container.

Boil the milk in the microwave briefly for about 1 minute

Allow foam to form on the mixture by stirring or blending.

Place the syrup at the bottom of the glass and add espresso and skimmed milk.

Sprinkle with whipped cream and the pumpkin pie spice.

RASPBERRY SWIRL POUND CAKE

Preparation Time: 2 hours

Servings 10

Ingredients

For the pound cake:

- 1 box mix of Pound Cake
- ¼ cup of butter (tender)
- 2 eggs
- ⅔ cup of milk

- 1 tsp. of lemon juice
- 1 cup of seedless raspberries
- 6 drops of red food coloring (optional)

For the icing
- 8 cups of cream cheese (tender)
- 1 cup of powdered sugar
- 1 tsp. of lemon juice

Directions
Preheat the oven to 665 °F
Oil and flour 9x5 baking dish.
Add the cake, milk, egg and bread mixture, then shake gently until it is mixed (30 seconds).
Beat for an average of 2 more minutes.
Transfer the batter to another bowl.
Place the raspberry stamp and food coloring in a new bowl and stir well.
Whole lemon juice is boiled first and mixed well.
Add a white layer of batter to the pan.
Include alternating red and white layers.
Then bake for about 55 minutes
Remove from the oven and allow to cool.
Beat cream cheese over medium-low and low heat (4-5 minutes).
Mix the powdered sugar and stir until they stick. Add lemon juice mixed at a low level until it evenly blend.

STRAWBERRIES AND CREME FRAPPUCCINO

Preparation Time: 25 minutes

Servings 3

Ingredients

- ½ cup of milk
- ¼ glass of vanilla ice cream
- 1 cup of ice cream
- 2 berries
- 2 tbsp. of syrup, strawberry flavor
- ⅛ tsp. of Xanthan Gum (optional)
- Whipped cream

Directions

Mix all ingredients except whipped cream in a food processor. Add process well till all the ingredients are evenly mixed Transfer the mix to a serving glass and pour the whipped cream over it.

CHAPTER 9:

OTHER COPYCAT RECIPES

CHIPOTLE COPYCAT RECIPES

CHIPOTLE VINAIGRETTE

Servings 32
Preparation Time: 5 minutes;

Ingredients

- 1 tsp. of garlic powder
- 1 tsp. of cumin
- 1 tbsp. of salt
- 1½ tbsp. of black pepper
- 1 tsp. of oregano leaf
- ⅓ cup of stevia liquid
- ½ cup red wine vinegar
- 1½ cup of avocado oil
- 1 tbsp. adobo sauce
- 1 tbsp. of water

Directions

Turn on the food processor, add all ingredients except oil, cover with a lid, and then pulse for 30 seconds until even and smooth.

Mix with a constant oil flow until it is emulsified, then put the salad dressing into a medium bowl.

Serve immediately.

Nutritional information

103 Cal; 11.5 g fat; 0.05 g protein; 3.05 g net carbohydrates; 0.05 g of fiber;

SWEET CHILI SAUCE

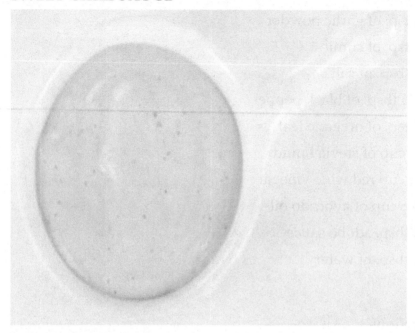

Servings 6

Preparation Time: 5 minutes

Cooking time: 15 minutes

Ingredients

- 1 tbsp. of garlic and chili sauce
- ½ cup of water
- 2 tbsps. of collagen from beef bone broth
- ¼ a glass of rice vinegar without salt
- 1 tsp. of garlic powder
- ¼ tsp. of ground ginger
- ¼ cup erythritol sweetener
- 1 tbsp. of avocado oil

Directions

In a large bowl, add all ingredients except oil and shake until everything is mixed evenly.

Take a medium-sized saucepan, place it on a stove of medium heat, add the sauce mixture and then let it simmer for 15 minutes until the sauce thickens.

When finished, remove the pan from the stove, stir in the oil, allow the sauce to cool completely, and then serve.

Nutritional information

25 cal; 2.2 g fat; 0 g protein; 1.2 g net carbohydrates; 0 g of fiber;

BANG BANG SAUCE

Servings 6

Preparation Time: 5 minutes

Cooking time: 0 minutes

Ingredients

¼ cup of mayonnaise

1½ tbsp. of garlic and chili sauce

1 tbsp. of white vinegar

2 tbsps. of fruit sweetener

⅛ tbsp. salt

Directions

Turn on the food processor, add all the ingredients, cover with a lid, and then pulse for 30 seconds until smooth.

Pour the sauce in a bowl and serve.

Nutritional information

90 Cal; 10 g of fat; 0 g protein; 1 g net carbohydrates; 0 g of fiber;

CARAMEL SAUCE

Servings 12
Preparation Time: 5 minutes
Cooking time: 15 minutes

Ingredients

- 3 tbsps. of erythritol sweetener
- 1 tsp. of vanilla extract, unsweetened
- ⅓ cup butter, salted
- ⅔ cups of cream

Directions

In a medium-sized saucepan, place on a low heat, add butter and erythritol, then cook for 4 to 5 minutes until the butter melts and turns golden brown.

Stir the cream, bring to a boil and then simmer the sauce for 10 minutes until the sauce covers the back of the spoon, stirring constantly.

Remove the pan from the heat, stir in the vanilla extract and serve.

Nutritional information

91 Cal; 10 g of fat; 1 g protein; 0 g without carbohydrates; 1 g of fiber;

POPEYE COPYCAT RECIPES
POPEYES CHICKEN STRIP

Servings 6

Preparation Time: 10 minutes

Cooking time: 20 minutes

Ingredients

- 2 pound of chicken breast
- ⅔ cup of almond flour
- 2 tsps. of salt
- 1 tsp. of chili powder
- 2 tsps. of smoked paprika
- ⅓ cup of special hot sauce with low-carb
- 3 eggs
- ½ cup almond milk, unsweetened
- Avocado oil for frying

Directions

In a small bowl, pour the milk and stir in the hot sauce.

Cut each chicken breast into four pieces, place it in a large bowl, pour half of the milk mixture into it and soak for at least 1 hour.

Then take a flat plate, add flour and mix with salt, paprika and pieces while mixing.

Beat the eggs in the remaining milk mixture and then beat until it starts to foam.

When the chicken is marinated, drain well, put each piece of chicken into the flour mixture, dip it in the egg mixture, and put it again into the flour mixture.

When you are ready to cook it, take a large pot, fill it with 2 inches of oil, put the pan over a stove of medium heat, and bring butter to 360 °F.

Then dip the chicken piece into the oil, don't overfill and then fry on each side for 5 to 7 minutes until well fried and golden brown.

Remove from oil and transfer the pieces of chicken to the plate with a paper towel and repeat with the remaining pieces of chicken.

Serve immediately.

Nutritional information

385 Cal; 25 g of fat; 35 g protein; 4 g net carbohydrates; 1 g of fiber;

CALIFORNIA PIZZA COB SALAD AND RANCH DRESSING

Servings 2

Preparation Time: 10 minutes;

Ingredients

For the Ranch Dressing:

- 1 tbsp. of seasoning
- 3 tbsps. of mayonnaise
- 2 tbsps. of water

For salads:

- ½ pound of grilled chicken
- 3 ounces of cooked bacon
- 5 ounces chopped lettuce
- 1 medium tomato, chopped
- 1 medium peeled, pitted and chopped avocado

- 1 tbsp. minced garlic
- ½ tsp. of salt
- ⅓ tsp. black pepper
- 2 boiled eggs
- 2 ounces of crumbled blue cheese

Directions

Mix up the dressing by taking a small bowl, add all the ingredients and stir until evenly mixed.

Put the salad together and cut the chicken into small pieces and then divide it evenly in two bowls.

Remove the shell from the boiled egg, cut it into slices and divide it evenly in a salad bowl.

Mix the vegetables, cheese and bacon, season the salad with salt and pepper, then sprinkle the dressing that has been prepared on top.

Sprinkle with garlic and serve.

Nutritional information

945 Cal; 81 g of fat; 43 g protein; 6 g net carbohydrates; 9 g of fiber;

IN N OUT BURGER

Servings 5

Preparation Time: 10 minutes

Cooking time: 10 minutes

Ingredients

For Patties:

- 1½ pound of ground beef
- 1 tsp. of salt
- 1 tsp. of black pepper
- 5 pieces of American cheese

For sauce:

- ⅓ cup of mayonnaise
- 1 tbsp. of soy sauce, without sugar
- 1 tsp. of mustard paste
- 2 tbsps. of cucumber
- 2 tsps. cucumber juice
- ½ tsp. of salt
- ½ tsp. red pepper

- ½ tsp. of garlic powder

For dressing:
- 10 sliced tomatoes
- 20 lettuce leaves
- 10 pieces of cucumber
- ½ large garlic, peeled, cut into thin strands

Directions

Prepare the sauce by taking a small bowl, add all the ingredients and stir until mixed. Set aside as needed.

Prepare patties using a medium bowl, add beef, add salt and pepper, mix well and form a mixture into ten balls.

Take a frying pan and place on a stove to heat it on high heat, spread oil in the pan and when it is hot, add patties balls in it, flatten and fry on its side for 4 to 5 minutes until well fried and brownish.

When finished, place a piece of cheese on top of the patty and place another patty on top of the cheese and first patty, and repeat with the other patties.

Put together the burgers and use two lettuce leaves as the base part of the bun, add a few slices of onion, topped with stacked patties and then add two slices of each pickles and tomatoes.

Spread the prepared sauce on the patties and cover it with two lettuce leaves.

Put together the remaining burgers in the same way and serve.

Nutritional information

696 Cal; 49.5 g fat; 52.2 g protein; 6.5 g net carbohydrates; 4 g fiber;

PARMESAN PORK CHOPS

Servings 2

Preparation Time: 5 minutes

Cooking time: 10 minutes

Ingredients

- 4 boneless pork chops
- ½ tsp. of garlic powder
- ¼ tsp. of salt
- ¼ tsp. of white pepper
- 2 tbsps. of avocado oil
- 1 egg
- 4 ounces of grated parmesan cheese

Directions

In a small bowl, add garlic powder, add salt and pepper. Stir until everything is mixed.

On both sides of the pork, sprinkle the spice mixture and press it with little pressure.

In a flat plate, break the eggs in it and beat the whites.

In a separate flat bowl and place parmesan cheese on it.

Dip each slice of pork in the egg, then cover it with cheese.

In a frying pan add oil and put it on stove of medium heat, and when it is hot, add the prepared pork and fry it 5 minutes to the side until brown and soft.

When done, transfer the pork to a plate and repeat with other pork chops indiscriminately.

Serve immediately with cauliflower puree.

Nutritional information

370 Cal; 26 g fat; 32 g protein; 1 g net carbohydrates; 0 g of fiber;

RED LOBSTER COPYCAT RECIPES
SHRIMP SCAMPI

Servings 4

Preparation Time: 5 minutes; Cooking time: 10 minutes;

Ingredients

- 1¼ pound of shrimp, tail removed and stripped
- 1½ tbsp. of minced garlic
- 2 sliced scallions
- ¾ tsp. of salt
- ½ tsp. of black pepper
- ¼ tsp. of red pepper flakes
- ¼ a bowl of chopped parsley
- 4 tbsps. of butter, tasteless
- ¼ glass of lemon juice
- ¼ a glass of Chardonnay
- ½ cup of grated parmesan cheese

Directions

In a large saucepan, place on a stove of medium heat, add butter and when it melts, add garlic and cook for 1 minute until soft and golden brown.

Add the shrimps, cook for 3 to 4 minutes until they become pink, then use a pair of tongs to turn the shrimp over, sprinkle with paprika flakes, and continue cooking for 3 minutes.

Then add the lemon juice to the shrimp, cook a little longer, then remove the pan from the heat.

Sprinkle shrimp with scallions and parsley, season with salt and pepper, then add cheese.

Serve immediately.

Nutritional information

332 Cal; 17 g of fat; 34 g protein; 7 g net carbohydrates; 1 g of fiber;

CHEDDAR BAY BISCUITS

Servings 9

Preparation Time: 10 minutes

Cooking time: 11 minutes

Ingredients

- 1½ cup of almond flour
- 1 tsp. of garlic powder
- ¼ tsp. of salt
- 1 tbsp. of baking soda
- ½ cup grated cheddar cheese
- ½ cup of sour cream
- 4 tbsps. of butter, unsalted
- 2 eggs

About the toppings:

- ½ tsp. of garlic powder
- 2 tbsps. of butter, unsalted
- 1 tbsp. of parsley powder

Directions

Turn on the oven, set it to 450 °F and let it heat up first.

In a large bowl, add flour and mix with garlic, baking soda, and salt until they have fused together.

In a small bowl, beat the eggs, beat the butter and sour cream until it is smooth, then stir the almond flour mixture until the smooth mixture is collected.

In a muffin can with 12 cups, rub the cup with oil, fill it evenly with the dough, then bake for 11 minutes until the top of each biscuit turns golden brown and toothpicks are inserted into each biscuit for it to come out clean.

Meanwhile, take a small bowl, add melted butter, stir the garlic powder until it dissolves, then stir the parsley.

When finished, remove the biscuits from the baking pan, place them on a baking sheet, and immediately sprinkle garlic and parsley butter on each biscuit.

Serve immediately.

Nutritional information

240 cal; 22 g of fat; 7 g protein; 3 g net carbohydrates; 0.5 g of fiber;

FISH AND CHIPS

Servings 2

Preparation Time: 15 minutes

Cooking time: 30 minutes

Ingredients

For chips:

- 1 medium sized zucchini
- ¼ tsp. of salt
- ¼ tsp. of black pepper
- ½ tbsp. of avocado oil

For fish:

- ¾ pound of codfish
- ½ cup almond flour
- ¼ tsp. of onion powder

- ½ tsp. of salt
- ⅓ tsp. black pepper
- ½ tsp. of paprika powder
- 4 cups of avocado oil
- 1 egg
- ½ cup of grated parmesan

For dipping sauce:
- ¼ tbsp. of curry powder
- 2 tbsps. of delicious pickles
- ½ cup of mayonnaise

Directions

Prepare the sauce for dipping by taking a medium bowl, add all the ingredients, stir until thoroughly mixed, and set aside until needed.

Turn on the oven, set it to 400 °F and let it heat up first.

Then chop the zucchini into thin stripes, put it in a medium-sized bowl, coat with oil, then stir until entirely coated.

Place the zucchini strips on a baking sheet, season with salt and pepper, then bake for 30 minutes until they are golden brown.

Then prepare the fish by break eggs in a flat bowl and then beating white.

In a separate flat bowl, add flour, add all the spices and cheese, and stir until evenly mixed.

Cut the shells into 1 x 1 inch, dip each part in the almond flour mixture, dip it in the eggs, then sprinkle the almond flour mixture again.

In a large pot, place on a stove of medium heat, add oil, heat for 12 minutes until it reaches 360 °F, then add pieces of fish that have been prepared and fry for 4 minutes for the sides to evenly turn golden brown and crispy.

Distribute the baked zucchini evenly on two plates, add fried fish and serve with dip sauce.

Nutritional information

884 Cal; 70 g fat; 51 g protein; 10 g net carbohydrates; 5 g of fiber;

CONCLUSION

In terms of health, cost, and overall enjoyment and pleasure, copycat recipes for the home have the full advantage to eating fast food in restaurants. If you stray from fast food in a restaurant for a long time, you might even stop eating expensive restaurants dishes.

Eating well is perhaps the most ideal way to feel better on busy days and maintain a high standard of living. Try it for half a month. You will definitely see its benefits soon.

I hope this book shows you how to make homemade dishes using copycat recipes. What are you waiting for? Go straight to the grocery store and try them, and I guarantee you won't regret.

Thanks for reading!

Please add a short review on
Amazon
and let me know your thought!

davidkern488@gmail.com

Made in the USA
Las Vegas, NV
08 December 2023

82371289R00090